BURN DOWN THE ICONS

Princeton Series of Contemporary Poets

THEODORE WEISS, EDITORIAL ADVISER

OTHER BOOKS IN THE SERIES

Atlantic Wall, by Rosalie Colie
Returning Your Call, by Leonard Nathan
Sadness And Happiness, by Robert Pinsky

Burn Down the Icons

POEMS BY

GRACE SCHULMAN

Princeton University Press

PRINCETON, N.J.

Copyright © 1976 by Princeton University Press

Published by Princeton University Press, Princeton, New Jersey
In the United Kingdom: Princeton University Press, Guildford, Surrey

ALL RIGHTS RESERVED

Library of Congress Cataloging in Publication Data will
be found on the last printed page of this book

Publication of this book has been aided by a grant
from the Paul Mellon Fund

This book has been composed in Linotype Granjon

Printed in the United States of America
by Princeton University Press, Princeton, New Jersey

ACKNOWLEDGMENTS

These poems first appeared in the following publications:

Poetry: "The Examination: Remembrance of Words Lost," "Tree of Life" and "That Maple."

Poetry Northwest: "Street Dance in Barcelona" and "Shango Sacrifice."

The Nation: "The Abbess of Whitby," "The Border," "In the Police State," "In the Country of Urgency, There is a Language," "Cold Fire" and "Morning Song."

American Poetry Review: "Burn Down the Icons," "Written on a Road Map" and "Poetry Editor."

The Hudson Review: "Metamorphosis," "Lost Unity," "Moon," "Recovery" and "The Other Side of Humankind."

Antaeus: "Birds on a Blighted Tree."

The Ohio Review: "Names" and "Application."

The Beloit Poetry Journal: A Chapbook for David Ignatow: "Double Vision" and "Waking a Soul in a Tree Near West House."

New Letters: "Epithalamion."

The Humanist: "Surely as Certainty Changes" and "Horses on the Grass."

"The Other Side of Humankind" was reprinted in *New American Poetry Into the Eighties: The Doctor Generosity Poets*. An early version of "Burn Down the Icons" appeared as a pamphlet, printed by The Seafront Press, Dublin.

"The Other Side of Humankind," "Lost Unity" and "Metamorphosis" were translated into Turkish by Talat Sait Halman. The first two versions appeared in *Varlık*, the third in *Sesimiz* (Istanbul, Turkey).

With gratitude to
The Corporation of Yaddo
The MacDowell Colony
AND
The Michael Karolyi Memorial Foundation
where many of these poems were written,
AND TO THE
P. E. N. American Center, for
the Lucille J. Medwick Memorial Award

To Jerome Schulman and for
Marcella and Bernard Waldman

CONTENTS

V. BURN DOWN THE ICONS

I. DOUBLE VISION

Morning Song

Love, we have lain awake all night
Talking of *aubades*, in this country
Where lovers died to live. Our moment fails
Outside the stone home. Morning,
And cocks whistle "La Marseillaise."

Dense ghosts crowd the sense
That would see things whole:
Where that day waned, our air is flung
With forms that change;
We burn on air as fire feeds and kills,
As water becomes ice or vapor,
As sun moves all things,
We manage mountains,
Altering horizons.

Yet even here,
The limestone rocks are skulls,
The river we cannot see
Sings us awake. Your face broods
Across olive wood.

Love, like these ancient trees
We stand apart
But meet, bend and protect,
Then gaze out at the world
In the same way.

Double Vision

In that place there are no atlases,
No lighthouses, no laws. No gravity.
The saints unsanctified,
My language lies undone.

My arms are seared with numbers and my hands
Detonate when they reach out.
Circles read "You Are Here"—there.

It is a black arrow trembling in a yellow diamond;
"What is it?" he screamed, his eyes were fallen rocks;
"Danger," I replied.
"You're wrong," he said. "It is an arrow."

Dreamless I ran unsteadied in that night
And prayed for tolerant winds to sing me home,
But I would set my stores by that disordered ocean.

Eyes be my images
O fire I fear
I am the star in the East
I rise in dry places and fall knowing

My heart's arhythmia, my double vision
Are handicaps. They are all I have.
I am at the bottom of that rock
From which altars are built.

Lost Unity

Worlds born again
In thunder, I see darkly,
My wholeness gone, how vulnerable
It is.

I am grass that has taken the form
Of your body where it has lain, losing
All other forms; and every face
Breeds yours in my quick eyes.
I lie halved: my body strives for you
As roots struggle for earth.
I remember a starfish
I lifted out of the sea, rays
Lowering tiers of hollow feet
That grasped for water. I let it go,
My hand a star.

Metamorphosis

I

See me in the glaze
On a leaf, in the skin's
Iridescence, have me in luminous
Reveries; light turns into me.
I preside the sea: waves harness
My force. I am lightning
Flashing; I am the lair
Of all change that is life.
My road is various; an alternating blaze;
I generate and destroy,
Feed what I devour,
Burning on air.

II

Roaring in the night for thousands of miles
I do not sing with flames.
I, too, change—into swirling clouds, into vapor;
Winds send foam rolling over me,
Marble sheets in my wake.
Life begins and ends here: large with rain,
I hold generations.
I break through rock, pour over sand,
Flow below ice, above tides,
Thunder under lightning,
Juggle blades in air;
I crash myself out in phosphorescent spray whispering
I shall be there when waves pass by.

III

Forced up by earth,
Cracked by ice,
I am the mountains and the valleys.
Even the wind will age in me.
I fall for centuries before I shine,
A meteor—a slow dream coming in

Surely as Certainty Changes

Surely as certainty changes,
As tide moves sand,
As heat sends wind to force the sea into waves,
As water rises and returns in rain
Or circles into smoke and falls in vapor,
You are enchanted for you enter change
And change is holy.

As earth's weight compresses rocks
Under trees over time, you enter change,
I know your face gives light as I know fire
Alters everything,
And falls rising,
Feeds and nourishes, opens and closes.

I pray to Proteus, the god of change
And proteolysis, "the end of change
Changing in the end"
To break old images and make you new
As love is its own effect unendingly.

The Other Side of Humankind

For Countess Catherine Karolyi, Vence

These are the hills of healed divisions;
The river we cannot see sings us awake,
Parting the mountains. I am familiar
With trees at false distances
In the clear air.

Remembering maps whose boundaries
Were scars, stitches
Of broken lines,
We grow whole—a continent
Of one color.

Twisted oaks hide
A rectangle reading,
In lapsed letters,
Chasse Interdite,
And all roads lead
To the sign
That cannot be seen.

Here, the river swims us;
We shine at moons.
Clouds whiten dark skies,
Light rings horizons after nightfall
That never seems to fall;
An ancient olive branch screens
Older stars.

Exiles, we have crossed
The solid white line
Between countries and loves
And torn selves,
Losing borders,
Questioning frontiers.

But see! Limestone terraces
Are a wall of skulls
That part like seas when you climb them,
Revealing trees,

And you stand
On your stone balcony
Framed in your chancel window,
Commanding even shadows to shed their provinces
And nightingales to sing beyond confusion.

II. WAITING FOR A COMET

Poetry Editor

Caught on a traffic island
in Park Avenue, I waited,
staring at dahlias,
cars enclosing me in a moving
parenthesis, red lights
arresting me. The stranger came,
wary, lizardlike, observing me
observe him, pressing pages
in my hand: "I want to talk with you
about matters of interest
to both—my poetry."
                    "Of course."
From a drawer with grooves
for silver needles, my dentist
reached for metaphors.
                    "Oh yes,
of course."

And when my neighbor
at a farmhouse in the pines
lodged notes he thought I had not seen
beneath my breakfast plate, I said again
"Of course."
Day of Atonement: in the house of God
trumpets began an elusive,
uncertain staccato flourish;
then, the horn stuttered
that once woke me
to song: "Let mountains rise
to trumpets throughout the land."
Trembling to that blare, I saw
a choir angel flutter
a white arm that implored me
to hear his cadences.
Wavering, I whispered
"Of course."
And yet again
of course. For, day by day, those images
rise like smoke, turn like a windmill,
furnish a beehive
I have not arranged; I never know
when fire in some unlikely place
will seize me; when my ears will reel
to that elusive music.

                    Worn at last,
I flew to Antibes and, one day,
swimming toward me,
under a snorkle,
a masked man cried "*Attends!*"
his manuscript translated
into English lying
on black stones.
                    "*Bien sûr*," I said,
as on the traffic island.
I, too, look for mail.
And when green signals tell me to, I cross
Park Avenue,
waiting for a comet
to flare suddenly
firing
my landscape
of bricks and glass.

Application

Five-feet-eleven and three-quarters inches
of nervousness. My arms are crazed antennae, and my voice
is crepitant. Love's scars are handicaps.
My life work? Life. Experience? These dotted lines
converge. Criminal offenses? Love.
I immolate myself, betraying friends
(my enemies), decoding messages,
crossing vein-shaped boundaries without visas.
Like Dante's damned, I see the future
but not the past. Always I return
to that disordered sea, finding
no safety zones and no
unwavering shorelines, my language failed,
silent in sourceless lightning,
mending my wind-split craft.
I am guilty of loving within perforated lines,
in shaded areas, in corners marked
"For official use only."

The Examination: Remembrance
of Words Lost

—What happened at your orals, Grace?
Taking a pipe from a row of suckling pigs, the chairman swung
In his chair. An A-shaped face, kind voice. Eyes, rubber stamps:
Failure. Special case.

        —I lose it now,
But I will try to call it back. Dim stars
That fade to a stare can shine at a backward glance.

—Why did you fail?

        —I did not. Words failed *me*
When I heard words about words, and swallowed tides
Of questions, as rock-hollows suck sea.

—Why are you here?

        —A star once summoned me,
As gravity pulls others to the ground.
That star is light-years distant from me now,
But still it burns, unseen, waiting to shine.
I wait for syllables to fall. Or burn, like ice.

—Good answer, though your style is hard to follow.
Have you tried aeronautics? Astro-physics?
These numbers: Ninety percent of you are brainless,
My records show, though eighty-six percent
Pass on the second try. But you—good teacher,
Student, lover of words. What happened, Grace?

—They led me to a room with a womb-shaped table
On which my fathers laid twelve hands. Six scraped faces nodded.
Above, fluorescent rectangles were frozen lakes
Of corrugated glass. The walls were soundproof.
I greeted a darning-egg.

                            —We haven't met
Officially.

            Mist fell. Tide went over me.

—In eighteen-eighty, where would you buy a book?

—At the corner of Third and Bleecker, in ribs of sun,
Where I left my mind.

                            Their voices bonged
Contrapuntally:

                            —The chicken or Emily Dickinson?
The egg enjoined. Another:

                            —Stephen or Hart?
Henry or William? I did not know
Which of his heads to answer. Totem pole
Of painted masks gone white.

A man with a face like a dime on edge said,
Fields away,

—Was there a real
House in Albany? His headlights caught my eyes.

—There was. I lived there once. But I can't recall
Where Henry was when William was at Harvard.

Their voices thrummed:
                    —Internal evidence? —Any sex
In Sextus Propertius?

                —Elders, let me finish
Bathing. I am no exhibitionist . . .

When Caedmon turned from song to sing
Hild made him monk, but only after
God made him poet—and I think his God
Was some dark, fierce power that forced up his song.
I cannot tell you how he sang, how syllables
Danced from a man who could not read.

                        —A monk?
Oh, yes. Of course. But nowadays we can't
Give Ph.D.s for *that*. What's your profession?

—Poet.

  —Published poet?

      —Yes.

                     —Well, *poetry*
Has nothing to *do* with scholarship. Your sentence:
A year of failure and a crown of silence.

Five fathers vanished. One remained.

                        —My friend,
I see you have been walking under water.
Look upward now.

                I surfaced then, saw shadows
That had been knives, and moved into myself.

In the Country of Urgency,
There is a Language

(*To Marianne Moore*)

> *"Ezra Pound said never, NEVER to use*
> *any word you would not actually say in*
> *circumstances of utmost urgency."*

I

"Can you hear me? I talk slowly now,"
You said, months past. "When Ezra Pound
Came, he could not say a word."
When your voice waned, I prodded syllables,
Examined frequencies, listened for cadences,
Demanding clarity. Sounds inconceivable
Have meaning now. Four heavy stresses:
"How is your work?" Light syllables:
"Do I look well?" Fire-forced speech
Caught, wordless. It will suffice.

II

December 22, 1970

In the country of urgency, there is a language
I hear as I follow the fall of your hand
And a blue light from the door of your dark apartment.
Your body vanishes behind bedrails.
Your hand I can't let go flows into me.

Blue eyes burn images in me. Those images,
Those sounds, those necessary gestures
Are a language. They will suffice.

III

No note from you. Remembering your leopard,
"Spotted underneath and on its toes,"
And how you'd said, "a leopard isn't spotted
Underneath, but in the tapestries it is,
And I liked the idea," I brought the photograph
Of leopards spotted everywhere. Home from the hospital,
Immobile, in a billowing blue gown,
You stalked those beasts and raised yourself in bed:
"Those are cheetahs, Grace!" and lay down again.

IV

Your silence is a terrible fire in me that sings on to be fed,
A musical wind that splits my craft, hail-hard, that lashes me
    dumb.
It is a strange country. Where are the maps,
The lighthouses, the gyroscope you gave me
That rights itself in motion? I have forgotten my name
As well as the irregular conjugations I memorized.
Occasionally, though, a blue light flashes directions
Over dangerous shale, and I hear you
Over protest shouts, explosions, immolations,
Over unreliable telephone connections, I hear you
Over labels, over a broken air conditioner, a plane;
I hear you over the silences we call conversation.
Your voice rolls in me thunder in a night of invisible stars,
And I wake to the sounds of your silence. They are a language.
                        They will suffice.

" 'Fool,' Said my Muse to Me,
'Look in thy Heart and Write' "

Imagine finding there a lantern
of fluted glass; consider mining
that pit and digging loose a hammered bowl,
a stereopticon with slides of the Alhambra.
I dredged that swamp and surfaced, clutching
metal sconces, grasping
brass decanters.

          In that place
light was a meteor
burning into sight near earth's orbit;
the sun grew rectangles beyond the trees
and struck glass sapphire and amber.
Nothing was fixed. My so-called heart
leaped at the sight of oaks,
cartwheels of palms,
grave hemlocks.
          I moved through time and gathered
Chatham watches under glass; I scanned dark walls,
saw rising over me
a terra cotta nun, an eyeless portrait
of Edgar Allan Poe.

Fishing that well
I caught bulrushes and lichen,
death's-head
hawk moths,
fish blowing reedy notes. My heart's
a junk shop of disguises.
                    Rising then,
I served the oriole I did not see,
the sun that purified rivers
and fired the moon.

III. NAMES

Birds on a Blighted Tree

Free things are magnets to the moving eye,
Beckoning the mind to rouse the dead;
Under a cloud's passing power
A spire sails—a mast.
These birds antagonize a tree:
Scavengers invade decay
Winter's engraved in air.
Defiantly they strain for light and fly,
Tightening branches to bows.
Iconoclasts impress indelible
Veronicas on living things,
Leaving a branch leafless.
Free things breed freedom;
That dead arm beating.

Names

"This is ozone," you said,
staring at absolute air,
startled by all things
palpable, familiar;
the less we know
about a thing, the more
names we give it.
Nominal friend,
I find you in rain,
see you in waves that radiate
rainbows,
your voice in my quick
ears, inventing
hemlocks, rose-breasted
grosbeaks. Even now,
this weedy grove spins
starflowers, *arbor
vitae*, aspens
and foamflowers
(one word);
from the bottom
of your word-hoard,
names govern the world.

Waking a Soul in a Tree
Near West House

The bark of your face
Ages in this tree,
Your light beams through it;
Knots ripple out,
Eyes, first circles, see.

Horses on the Grass

From the tower window
the moon
draws a silver-maple's shadow
across a spangled lawn;
              horses
rear, manes lashing the air,
front legs floating.
             Half monarch,
half shadow, the tree
aspires to the sky;
one branch, cracked by lightning
scrapes the earth.
          Reflected
on the grass, bent twigs
are curved hooves, galloping
as the moon rises.

Divided it stands
in wholeness, mourning
its victories, praising
the god of trees, the king of horses.

The tree holds souls
in a bark prison
poised like a runner at the starting line—
and bolts free, wildly
pawing the ground those roots lie under.

That Maple

You are right, that maple ruined
the landscape; it was out of place.
How it stood in the middle of things,
hunched on the lawn screening
a marble nymph, her raised arms
making circles in water.
Out of the far reach of the eye
I never saw its branches; eyes rose over them
to mountains, painting images
on spindly twigs.
              You know trees
as they are; I gave one leaves
and dressed it in gold
like a love. I remember
a musical wind,
the crash-on-crash
of thunder; I never saw
lightning vein sky silver
and crack a branch
that lashed the lawn
and tracked earth
like the heart.

Tree of Life

If you can't see the wood for me
So much the better. Tiers of needles
Depend from arms that make arcs
When the wind disturbs them.
My hands command.
Even in this hairy grove
I cast tatterdemalion shadows
Changing as air plays taut strings.

I have deadly names:
Hemlock, white pine, *Arbor
Vitae* (tree of life
Meaning no life);
I hold souls that wake
When you pass.
Do not enter my husk,
My veins burrow underground
In dendrons and rivulets.
Through leaded triangles
Of mullioned glass,
My charred legs claw the earth.

The Abbess of Whitby

There must have been an angel at his ear
When Caedmon gathered up his praise and sang,
Trembling in a barn, of the beginning,
Startled at words he never knew were there.

I heard a voice strike thunder in the air:
Of many kings, only one god is king!
There must have been an angel at his ear
When Caedmon gathered up his praise and sang.

When Caedmon turned in fear from songs of war,
Gleemen who sang the glories of the king
And holy men wondered that so great a power
Could whirl in darkness and force up his song;
There must have been an angel at his ear
When Caedmon gathered up his praise and sang.

Whitby Abbey

Whitby Abbey rots like a skull
Where hairy horizons spin draggled
Trees. Black fragment on white sky,
Those sockets once held stained-glass eyes;
Now black birds thread white hollows.

The moors are a lunar country.
Lifeless above my head,
Hills revolve while I lose my way in craters,
Tatterdemalion heather, iridescent grass,
Crags at false distances and
Blackface sheep. Strange swamps threaten
Less than confusion. Eyes drift skyward
(No houses, birds, flowers)
Anchored, caught in

The death's-head.
Legend or truth?
I know now
Caedmon sang here.

Epithalamion

Look there! *The Lovers
In the Flowers.*
Chagall's lovers, forever
Ungoverned by gravity,
Surface the air
Like water, or
Lean on lilacs
Above a moon,
Over the distant
Fragment of a castle.
Is it fantasy? Hands,
Faces, arms
Are real, but made
Of smoke: sometimes,
In wind,
It skims the earth
But always rises.

Poem I Dreamed During a Year of Silence

I

Dead flowers in a jar on this stone;
Summer and all the rains are gone.

II

Rivers burn;
And these formless, capricious ghosts
Breathe and return.

IV. WRITTEN ON A ROAD MAP

Written on a Road Map

This chapel stands between Morgan and Dol
Inside the gargoyle's head of Brittany
Where towns are pale gray names and roads are numbers;
Nameless, deserted; it is closed for August.

But how the shadows of a calvary
Move like quick puppets managed by the sun;
In the yard, a soldier's name is cut on stone,
His life, in numbers, and a word, *Regrets*.

Barbara of the storm, John of the sea,
Saint Catherine fix me here, your fire my fire,
Establishing a chapel on a map
To stop the blur of trees, the flow of roads.

The Border

Two countries were divided by the sound
Of guns that sang all night along the border.
Morning: the countries had two colors,
As on a map; one side was dry as sand,
The other green. The border reappeared
Like a watermark of waves washed on the shore
By a surf that had been wild the night before.
The two sides were as silent as the day
An Israel moved into Jerusalem
Mourning for its faithless Absalom
Hung in the air for the wind to play.

In the Police State

Green lights grow from the trees in San Sebastian
To make the poplars greener than they are;
Along the waterfront, loudspeakers blare
Strauss cadences just as the night comes on.

Voices contend the martial sound, but slowly
Speech flickers and dies, and heels obey;
Anger: Flame quivers to survive the wind
As music drowns the sea and stills the mind.

This harbor's outsize arms contain the sea;
An Eden of green trees across the bay
Is an artifice of light. Such things compel
The burning eye as drums enclose the will.

We watch the pantomime of waves like thought
Made visible; we hear but do not hear
Voices go under the mutter of unseen trumpets.
The news is edited of wars; the air

Clean as these white streets. Waves gathering thunder
In silence, our mute voices fill with anger
Now and until the sun burns through these trees
And birds disturb the air with free, imperfect cries.

Shango Sacrifice

Singers accustomed to a wilder song
Gravely went down to the ascending waters;
Sleepwalkers all, they cast out voices, strong
Against the wind, compliant Jephthah's daughters
Proceeding; their white dresses skimmed the sand;
They shouted hymns and quarreled with the sea;
As on a night beyond their memory
The white bird struggled in a prophet's hand.

Silent men made sacrificial fires;
A white dress fluttered downward, whitening
The sand: black women chanting still,
Their harmonies precise as any choir's,
I watched them as a deaf man watches lightning—
A young girl, struck by singing, cried and fell.

Street Dance in Barcelona

Alone, I watched the solemn dance begin,
Waking from a silence that deceives,
That turns footsteps, or the rustle of dry leaves
Into the clatter of a tambourine.

Their voices had been rattling that day,
Rapid as drumbeats, in the *Catalan*,
But a wilderness of hands reached toward the sun
Like wheatstalks risen from a ground of clay.

The crowd broke into perfect wheels, turning
To the stuttering of a wooden horn,
Quickened by the beating of the sun;
I had seen their angry faces burning.

Strangers, we stand alone but turn together
As vanes become a windmill in the wind;
One hand opens for another hand,
The wheel breaks only to include another.

Bill Flanagan at Maryknoll

"I'm sure it is a drag if you don't believe,"
You say at last, staring at absolute air.
Now you must rise at three o'clock for prayer,
And I remember, as I turn to leave,
The night you challenged probability,
Sending a penny dancing from your hand,
Waking to laws that tranquilize the mind:
Eight hours, a hundred heads. No miracle,
Question all earthly currency. You are
Startled by all things palpable, familiar.
Love, love is a drag if you don't believe . . .
And now you stiffen as you pass the chapel
Trailing your silent wonder and afraid,
Eyes low, of seeing higher than your God.

Troilus and Cressida
in Central Park

Troy burns in Central Park.
Night after cloudless night
Smoke-clouds grow into stark
Black palls from scars of light.

The moon strides like a lion
Behind Ionic bars;
Then death-cries to the stars.
The war's begun again.

Mad-eyed with clarity,
Staggering orderly mind,
Cassandra prophecies,
Firing the fire like wind.

"Troy burns! Let Helen go!
A war of love is a love
Of war." Before me now
(Cassandra come alive)

The geometric skyline
Goes under a hideous glow,
Troy and the world I know—
Those sycamores—are one.

Just as the waking dreamer
Confronts the dream, I wake
To rocks, planes, lake
And cry, "The world's on fire.

"The flames are real!" Smoke shadows
The moon and the M   ONY sign;
Darkly I cry again.
My voice drowns in applause.

Burial of a Fisherman in Hydra

The day time failed began as usual.
Seeing the sun strike mica on the rocks,
I raced down terraces, past white
Sea houses casting black trapezoids
To watch the nightboat stagger in.
No nightboat, but a strange gray cutter
Moved into the harbor, bringing a fisherman
Who died in Athens, in a hospital.
There was a priest, a brilliant procession
Balancing scalloped crosses; the bells
Brawled; his women were black birds
Ridding the pier of swimmers and fishermen.
Suddenly, as though we knew him well,
The people stood in a silent chorus
Until the last cross-bearer disappeared
Among the listed saint-heads in the chapel.
Shadows that had been knives on the ground
Grew as on a sundial, measuring
The light; we followed in suppliance,
Night crowding every gutter of the rock.
In another time we might have mourned
Fallen heroes, carried in from sea
But in the imagination of the living
The fall from glory is the fall from being.
Night comes; that is the mystery of day.

Tower Suite

My father asked me, "Why do you write soft-sell?"
Cutting soft sole. "To sow hard seeds," I said,
"And sell hard souls." Through *The Tower* window,
The Time-Life sign blinked Time-Life, Time-Life
Flashing
Its occulting lights
Above the city.

The Law

My grandfather's mind was a covered ark
with doors that sprang shut when the truth was in.
"Pines bend with winds that snap oak.
They stand who bend before God."

Curtains and an ornamental lock
can light the law, as black soil shines at night;
dazzled by that law, I stood in wonder,
and trembled in the shadow of his hands.

Standing beside him in the synagogue,
I turned and saw a cage of women's faces—
fish leaping in nets—and one of them
my face, when I grew higher than his shoulder.

Stained glass grew leaves of light across the floor;
I saw a various truth with radiant shadows:
"Fathers, forgive me. I cannot follow."

The Fall

From the edge of the cliff I see your image
Break through limestone, shatter rocks,
Lift skyward,
Roots cleaving mountain crevasses.

From the bottom of rock pools
Your eyes arrest me, the scored rock face
Your face. Fallen, you know
The self that dies when selves are born.

I have climbed terraces,
Espadrilles pressing points of stars,
To hear you have looked below and fallen,
Rising in air.

We struggle into life from stones in gullies,
Falling like waterfalls that never fall.

V. BURN DOWN THE ICONS

Recovery

Recovery: returning
to the village where forests
are spirals of fire, to climb
narrow roads and find that pine
torn by lightning, its branches holding
stars of needles that strain the sky,
pointing upward, stiff
as hands in prayer.

To return in silence; I have touched
the nightingale I cannot see,
crossing the river
that drives through rocks
and sings in my blood,
treasure of my being.

I remember how the surgeon smiled, masked
in green gauze. I woke to eyes
watching me through lenses; voices
saying it was over, murmuring
"recover."

Here I rise
with the mountains.
I have given my name
and my language
to the primitive saints
in the chapel. I live in their light
and see the faces of all people
as one face.

Love, there is a world of pain
where sun fires bricks and glass
slowly as a season. I cherish pain
for it stills the sky to a halt,
arresting night.
Here may I see
those shadows stagger
that etch the olive,
recover,
follow a sun that makes days
green as the beginning,
light as creation;
let the river return things whole
in exchange for what we have broken.

Burn Down the Icons

What happened to Cassandra? She who cried
In me "Love is war!" has died, loving.
And Daphne, whose flesh grew leaves?
Breasts now, and twig-shaped nerves.
Fathers, forgive me. It had to be.
I never promised to be Saint Veronica
When you pressed images on me, printed in blood
On a white scarf. Or when you carved me in marble,
And gazed into the dry wells of my eyes,
Did you think I would not dissolve?

Well, burn down the icons. I have moved
Out of the Prado. Your best fresco
Cracks from the ceiling. I have gone
Beyond my body, five-feet-eleven and three-quarters
Inches of tangled philodendron. I am water.

Call out the curia. Unsanctify me.
Erase my feast day from the calendar.
Shatter the stained-glass windows of my mind.
They were idolators who cut the palm,
Two anchors and an arrow on my tomb
Found in the catacombs. I am no martyr.

Love was my habit. I know my heart moved trees.
Love called my eyes to change things of this world.
But I did not believe it. And how could I persuade you
That those visions you admired were astigmatism.
Makers of images, what you created in me
I was. But see me new! My nipples are cathedrals,
My flesh is a miracle. I flow to the ocean
Where all the rivers of the earth come together.
My body is a holy vessel. I am fire and air.

Do not desert me now, although I pray
To a genital god, and have let blaze
Strange images, my means of transportation.
I have established my chapel in water.
I would move through mountains. But fathers,
Let me return to a safe harbor; like the waves'
Slate-sheets, crash in the jetties of your arms.

Cold Fire

How could I know
As wind hovered over me,
Heat insinuating where
Light could not go

That fire
Ungoverned by gravity
Caught, blazing
Through morning's haze,
Loud colors astounding me,

That I was a miner, exploring
Inner earth, stronger
Than eye's light;
To seize is to surrender,
To burn is to grow cold.

How could I know
That you were never
My torn half,
My other self,
My angel,

And that all things—
Copper, iron,
Even trees—
Radioactive, lose
Dead heat over time,
Only emotion, the cloud's
Deadly energy,
Lingers.

Moon

Having no fire of my own, I shine
But never burn. I receive the light.
Man and woman, I gather both
Inside of me, surviving darkness,
Changing to grow whole
Or starving
Into halves and quarters.
If I do not feed flames,
Transparent fragments linger
After daybreak
And for brief moments
I cover the sun.

Letter to Helen

(*For Dr. Helena Waldman-Gold, 1898-1943*)

I

Your face broods from a sepia photograph:
eyes light over cheekbones.
Helen, I cannot lose your indelible
name, although I lose
others of the time.
When acts burn, there are images,
icons of blood and sweat
printed on my mind.

I have to recreate
your deed from voices
in the quick ears
of the child I was, from Black Books
I was allowed *not* to read. I have to guess
you knew our law of invisible
light: "Therefore choose life
that thou and thy seed shall live."
We dance to songs
in a world below ice, below time,
sleepwalk to laws
that manage our acts. Living our law
and science, your faith,
condemned to die,
you leaped from a tower in Poland, your death
firing our lives.

II

For years I would lessen your nobility,
call it impulsive, plead
it was useless, say
the sudden splendid act is no great thing,
survival is; the steady patient choice
of rightness over time, and excellence—
patience, the hero's passion.

To yield is to come back, I said, as water
yields to cleave stone, as tide ebbs
to move shorelines. Awakening at last
in a strange country, sun-dazed, I knew
the world's calm when acts
are stilled. Storms coned inward,
I stared down wind that spiralled to an eye.
Grown clear with knowing,
I found myself to be the heart of the storm,
born of the same that war is born.
"Therefore choose life," I cried, for David wept
when Absalom was slain, his criminal,
his outlaw son, however hard
the King had danced before God,
the ark safe in Jerusalem,
he wept, knowing his dance
was death.

III

A transatlantic call, beamed from a satellite:
I asked him, "Will you say
Celan's 'Fadensonnen'? I cannot find
your version." Static then,
and speech with echoes: " 'there are
still songs to be sung . . . sung . . . sung . . .
on the far side
of mankind . . . kind . . . kind.'
Damn that echo!"
My friend, your quiet voice insists on peace,
like "Dona Nobis Pacem," an antiphonal
high mass with fugue-like shadows,
endlessly persisting,
whatever corpses lie outside
the sandcastle Gothic church.

IV

Blood forces up my praise.
I am a fountain, juggling blades
to God, while everywhere the dead
lie on the streets, in crevasses, in fields;
today a woman set herself on fire
(my lover told me, setting me on fire
only to grow cold),
her body charred, her flesh burned to a log,
fire flattened her mouth and slit her eyes.

Fire forces me. I shout my praise
to the other side of humankind,
my name a blue number burned
on forearms of the imagination.
Your name was, is, will be, Helen.
And you will come for years through blackened air.
Your name leaps out of fire—salamander,
name of fire and unharmed by fire.
That is what icons are, indelible
prints on the mind. Your image is a fresco
that will not come down
in dust. Because you lived your life I shine
in flames, burning but not consumed,
changing to be myself, as though if water burned
it would be water all the more.
Courage you gave me, Helen, and your name
draws me like fire.

Double Vision:

> I am at the bottom of that rock
> From which altars are built.

Ten Sonnets to Orpheus by Rainer Maria Rilke, tr. Robert Bly (Mudra/Zephyrus): "The water rises clear from the same rock/ that holds up the huge doors and the altars."

Letter to Helen:

> A transatlantic call, beamed from a satellite:
> I asked him, "Will you say
> Celan's 'Fadensonnen'? I cannot find
> Your version. . . ."

"Fadensonnen" ("Thread-Suns"), by Paul Celan, was translated into English by Michael Hamburger.

Library of Congress Cataloging in Publication Data

Schulman, Grace.
  Burn down the icons.

  (Princeton series of contemporary poets)
  I. Title.
PS3569.C538B8   811'.5'4   76-3016
ISBN 0-691-06317-6
ISBN 0-691-01330-6 pbk.